The Beatitudes

They spoke, I think, of perils past.
They spoke, I think, of peace at last.
One thing I remember:
Spring came on forever,
Spring came on forever.

VACHEL LINDSAY
"The Chinese Nightingale"

The Beatitudes
a contemporary meditation

George A. Buttrick

design and illustrations by Diana Blank

ABINGDON PRESS / nashville and new york

THE BEATITUDES

Library of Congress Catalog Card Number: 68-25366

Scripture quotations unless otherwise noted are from
the Revised Standard Version of the Bible, copyrighted
1946 and 1952 by the Division of Christian Education,
National Council of Churches, and are used by permission.

The lines from "The Chinese Nightingale" are re-
printed with permission of The Macmillan Company
from Collected Poems by Vachel Lindsay. Copyright
1917 by The Macmillan Company, renewed 1945 by
Elizabeth C. Lindsay.

The lines by W. H. Auden, pp. 59, 63, are from For
the Time Being, copyright 1945 by W. H. Auden. Re-
printed by permission of Random House, Inc., and
Faber and Faber, Ltd.

SET UP, PRINTED, AND BOUND BY THE
PARTHENON PRESS, AT NASHVILLE,
TENNESSEE, UNITED STATES OF AMERICA

For my grandchildren

    ANNE, PETER, KAREN, STEPHEN,

    HILLARY, JEANNE AND MICHAEL,

by whom "in all things I am instructed,"
though not always according to the Beatitudes,
but who are always my grateful joy

THE BEATITUDES ACCORDING TO MATTHEW

Blessed are the poor in spirit, for theirs is the kingdom of heaven.

Blessed are those who mourn, for they shall be comforted.

Blessed are the meek, for they shall inherit the earth.

Blessed are those who hunger and thirst for righteousness, for they shall be satisfied.

Blessed are the merciful, for they shall obtain mercy.

Blessed are the pure in heart, for they shall see God.

Blessed are the peacemakers, for they shall be called sons of God.

Blessed are those who are persecuted for righteousness' sake, for theirs is the kingdom of heaven.

Blessed are you when men revile you and persecute you and utter all kinds of evil against you falsely on my account. Rejoice and be glad, for your reward is great in heaven, for so men persecuted the prophets who were before you.

MATTHEW 5:3-12

THE BEATITUDES ACCORDING TO LUKE

Blessed are you poor, for yours is the kingdom
of God.

Blessed are you that hunger now, for you shall
be satisfied.

Blessed are you that weep now, for you shall
laugh.

Blessed are you when men hate you, and when
they exclude you and revile you, and cast
out your name as evil, on account of the
Son of man! Rejoice in that day, and leap
for joy, for behold, your reward is great in
heaven; for so their fathers did to the
prophets.

LUKE 6:20-23

THE WOES ACCORDING TO LUKE

Woe to you that are rich, for you have received
your consolation.

Woe to you that are full now, for you shall
hunger.

Woe to you that laugh now, for you shall mourn
and weep.

Woe to you, when all men speak well of you,
for so their fathers did to the false prophets.

LUKE 6:24-26

"Spring came on forever" could be our subtitle, for the dictionary defines "beatitude" as a "state of utmost bliss." "Blessed" nine times over is the governing word. It has gathered a pious tone in our time. For us "happy" might be better, except that it misses an implied congratulation in the original Greek. "Bravo-joy to the peacemakers!" might be a good alternative. Incidentally, and not so incidentally, unless we have peacemakers our planet may soon be silent, because lifeless, under the mushroom cloud of an atomic bomb. If you are already asking how "happy" can ever jibe with "mourn" or "persecuted," your kind

10

patience please. But only for a little time: our journey by editorial edict is hardly as long as a village street.

To Nietzsche the Beatitudes were a "slave morality." We half believe him. So we have marching men, assembly lines, and grey flannel suits. Who's "slave" now? It follows that Hitler would and did send a leather-bound copy of Nietzsche's works to Mussolini. Jesus is not slave: he is the only free man. Swinburne said a worse thing about him: "The world has grown grey from thy breath." But then Swinburne did not live to see our factories polluting both air and water. Christ does not turn earth grey; he fills it with sunlight.

The Beatitudes are not "teaching," not schoolroom stuff. They are not good advice, thank heaven. They are not a pious "thought for the day." And journalism, feeding on conflict and sensation, has no right so to use them. They are not a mere daydream; ghettos may be a nightmare and suburbs a mirage, but the Beatitudes are as real as the springtime. If our computers, laboratories, and guns were massed, they could not stop that April. Every dark banner converged on Calvary and was overthrown. This we shall know even though planetary cataclysm, some dark apocalyptic curse which we now invite, may meanwhile fall on us. Jesus is present in his Spirit. If you doubt it, read the Beatitudes again, and you will find yourself saying, "Suppose he is right!" So to the several joys.

Blessed are the poor in spirit . . .

"Blessed are the poor in spirit." That does not mean poor-spirited; it means the opposite of proud. We sing the "Magnificat" in Latin, which helps us to enjoy the music and sidestep the words: "He has scattered the proud in the imagination of their hearts, . . . and exalted those of low degree." The poor in spirit are the lowly-hearted, in the midst of a culture which in its pride almost worships itself. So the Beatitudes even in our churches have become pious aesthetics. When we read them, they do not move us; we quickly forget and turn to thank God, when we thank him at all, for our "prosperity," which is no cause for thanksgiving.

14

Luke's version is short and blunt: "Blessed are you poor." No, Jesus did not champion "houseless heads and unfed sides" except in indignation. Neither did he offer a consolation prize to the dispossessed; poverty is not blessed in itself; the poor can be both cruel and greedy. But by and large they know their need. They are less tempted to make themselves their own god, a blasphemy which often besets the proud. We say, "Blessed are the successful, the powerful, the rich," whereupon Jesus flatly contradicts us. If he walked from our slums to our suburbs, he would weep at both ends of the journey. In many an instance the rich do not possess anything: their affluence possesses them. Then they suffer hardening of the arteries of compassion. Our world might be happier if we all lived in small houses with real friendships. Then we in America might quit pouring men and money into the bloody morass of war and give our surplus cash to meet the vast and pitiable needs of folk in other lands.

"But what is wrong with proper pride?" we ask, and then quote Emerson's "Self Reliance." I am writing from a hospital bed where I have learned again that "valiant dust that feeds on dust" is not self-reliant, and that any pride is a tragicomic selling out to the devil. So Matthew's "poor in spirit," though it may be a later version, clarifies the meaning. The poor, exactly opposite to the proud, know that we are but pensioners of a world we did not and could not make. They know that our very awareness of distortion and death hints a "great white Throne," just as our knowledge of dark would be impossible if we had not first seen light. Thus God is always round about us. The poor stand incredulous before the conceit which proclaims "God is dead."

So to the deepest meaning of the first beatitude. In the Old Testament, Christ's Bible, "the poor" is often a synonym for those who wait on God. They know that "if God stopped breathing we would all vanish." So they pray and pray in solitude and in their modest company. Joseph and Mary were among the poor in spirit who were "waiting for the consolation of Israel" in Christ. By the same token "the poor" know their dependence on their neighbors. Not soon shall I forget my first and only ride in a jinrikisha. A human being between the shafts as if he were a horse! I could not "take it"; I got out and walked. "Well, it's his livelihood," said my guide. The self-made man—was there ever such a bore?—travels between God's mysteries of birth and of death on trails he did not blaze, eats food he did not grow . . . ; you complete the list if you can. He rides a jinrikisha and has no right to "take it" unless he takes also his turn between the shafts. "Good for the lowly folk!" may be title for the other Beatitudes, the white light which breaks into seven spectrum colors. Pride is the root transgression. Churches which are overbuilt and overbudgeted, and thus dependent on rich men, are not "happy." "Ah, Davie, Davie," said Dr. Johnson admiring the lavish furnishings in the dressing room of David Garrick, the famous actor, "these are the things which make death terrible!" He was wrong; they make life terrible.

We do not believe the first beatitude. Why pretend we do? We believe in our "gre-e-at nation" or "our gre-e-at technological progress." Can't you hear the "orators" at a political convention? We believe in our per capita wealth, a term which hides all the cruel disparities. The child minds who compose our cigarette ads are for us the real people. After all, they have an annual budget of about $600,000,000. The underpaid schoolteachers, to whom we entrust our children, are obviously "not getting anywhere." But in Dante's picture of hell the damned sang, for their purification: "Blessed are the poor in spirit."

As for the reward, "for theirs is the kingdom of heaven," we can postpone comment, for it repeats. But meanwhile this: it is not a reward, still less a Sunday school prize for good behavior. We think of eternity as beginning only when time ends, which is like saying of some nearby field that it has no horizon. Eternity fills time as creation fills our planet. It breaks through our ordinary day like a fountain, falls on us like sunlight, streams across us like a clearing wind. This "the poor" know. They are already in heaven—"theirs is the kingdom"—while the proud eke out a shallow, timebound life. "The poor" worship at a throne as lowly as a manger, as self-forgetting as a cross. They do not need to search for heaven; it has already found them, and through them heaven invades our proud society to save us from a never distant hell.

Blessed are those who mourn . . .

"Blessed are those who mourn." That's crazy, isn't it? But Jesus doesn't play with words. He would have us know that sorrowing people, if they are not proud rebels, are surprised by joy in the very midst of grief. Nobody escapes death, for death begins his pursuit the moment we are born, and always overtakes us. Some folks try to hide from death, though there is no hiding place. Some try to forget at the risk of stifling their compassion. Some regard death as "purely scientific" (that puerility is written in Corliss Lamont's The Illusion of Immortality). Some pretend that death is illusion though a stilled voice and the nearby

graveyard give them little comfort. Some hug their grief, unaware that self-pity is a form of pride. But a few, "those who mourn," bare their breasts to the spear and then for love's sake share their neighbors' grief. They accept sorrow in the faith that it hides a bright secret.

Our present world is not altogether callous, but its sympathies are short and soon spent. What of the Negro ghetto breaking into violence because of the white man's long indifference and contempt? What of television advertising which never stops, even when giving us the body count (as if men were geese or rabbits) in our *latest war? But the sensitive few still mourn. Their compassion nowadays takes a corporate cast because we live in a corporate world. Technology necessitates communalism (not communism), like it or lump it, so sympathy protests governmental inertia and supports public measures of goodwill. But this "mourning," the exposure of our nerve ends to the pain of mankind, cannot ignore the man next door. Wasn't there a Broadway drama about a man living in a high-rise apartment who by means of lip-reading learned the anxieties of people on the street and secretly helped them? No need for the lip-reading—there is sorrow enough plain*

23

to see on any street, to plead for sympathy. "Isn't it also true," some thoughtful reader asks, "that those who mourn live in pain for their own sins?" Yes, the fourth beatitude will bring us to that crux.

"They shall find consolation," says the New English Bible, but the older, "they shall be comforted," is just as true, the more especially because "comforted" originally meant "fortified." We need both versions: they shall be consoled and fortified. They seek no such favor, or their sympathy might become selfishness. They ask no explanation of sorrow; they know there is none for our poor mortal minds. They believe that patience for oneself and love for one's neighbor will yield their own answer. Dean Inge lost a tiny daughter to death's untimeliness. So he faced and described the alternatives to faith: "A microbe blindly following its instincts. . . . An enemy has done this." But his faith rode the storm. Then he wrote: "Bereavement is the deepest initiation into the mysteries of human life, an initiation more searching and more profound even than happy love. It brings the eternal world nearer."

That is what Christ said nearly two thousand years ago as he took upon himself all our sin and sorrow. So now we worship before an empty cross. What other faith has such insight or would ever dare such a talisman? Luke's addition to the second beatitude, "Woe to you that laugh now, for you shall mourn and weep," is Christ's pity, not his threat. Can't you hear the laughers of our world, surface people who live only for a good time? They shrink from sorrow's dark initiation and miss the hidden joy. According to an old story, angels also mourn, and only those who bathe their eyes in the pool of earth's weeping have the gift to sing in the celestial choir. Isn't it strange that sorrow should bring joy? But, then again, Christ said some very strange things.

Blessed are the meek . . .

"Blessed are the meek" seems to be upside-down nonsense, mocking nonsense when it continues, "for they shall inherit the earth." Can you possibly see that inheritance in New York City now or Chicago? The college professor said, "Christianity seems to be a kind of masochism." To which I: "The man who tries to grab the earth soon loses it, as witness the trampling of our wars, and so becomes an unintentional masochist." He replied, "I don't get it." An honest answer, for this beatitude on its face is a riddle! Clearly "meek" does not mean a doormat. Just as "poor" is the opposite of proud, "meek" is the opposite of aggressor. The meek are the _unrevengeful_ victims of the aggressor's pride and power.

Christ's daring word is this: "Good for you when you do not exploit your neighbors, but choose to live in mingled lowliness and reverence!" Yes, this is nonresistance, but not passive nonresistance, for it boldly claims God's invasions. It has its indignations, but even these are meek because they flame in behalf of trampled folk as Lincoln's indignation caught fire for the sake of the slaves. The point is this: Jesus did not crucify anyone; he chose to be crucified. Who, then, has conquered, Pilate or Jesus, the warriors killing one another or the quiet company of the gentle-hearted? By the verdict of any period in history the meek become "the terrible meek." So Charles Rann Kennedy has rightly written: "The meek, the terrible meek, the fierce agonizing meek, are about to enter into their inheritance." The go-getters in city and nation are doomed. They commit either fratricide or suicide, living and dying, inside and outside, because the earth is not ours: "It is his, and he made it."

The pushers and the conquerors along with the advertisers (the latter with their explosions in print or neon lights) laugh aloud at the third beatitude. But are they "happy"? No, they run scared from St. Francis with his poverty and prayers and a faith that for sheer gladness danced on many a village green, and secretly they envy him. Darwin cannot explain how cattle have survived the survival of the fittest, still less how trampled truth outlasts our rampant lies. "But," someone asks, "aren't the meek slaughtered?" Oh, yes, every Attila has them in his power. Or does he? Christ was slaughtered. Or was he? His gallows stands while the swords that could not kill him are now poor shadow swords.

"Blessed are the meek" is a white gauntlet flung down at the feet of our violent world. Actually more than this world is involved, for God is not a tin-pot god with no better kingdom than the local cemetery. "The meek . . . inherit the earth." They do not try to grab it; they know it is not theirs to grab. They are God's legatees. It is bequeathed to them in the will of the crucified Christ, through whom the world was made. You and I must not push this promise only into some future beyond death. Eternity is not the mere extension of time. It impregnates time and rules time in every here and now. The meek live both in time and eternity. They know already and shall soon more clearly know that "spring came on forever." Who are the meek in our time? The tramplers running amuck or marching with the marching crowd—or the man who goes to jail for conscience' sake? Time will tell. Yes, it will tell surprising truth, because time is held in eternity.

Blessed are those who hunger and thirst for righteousness . . .

"Blessed are those who hunger and thirst for righteousness." Luke's version is as abrupt as a blow on the face: "Blessed are you that hunger now," which does not mean that ragged hunger is fortunate, but rather that human need makes a man realize that human powers are never enough and thus opens the door to God. Luke's "Woe to you that are full now, for you shall hunger" neither threatens nor gloats; it is a profound sadness. It points to a worse famine described in a tremendous passage in Amos: "Not a famine of bread, nor a thirst for water, but of hearing the word of the Lord." Without that secret bread a man dies even

while he lives. Once I saw a man fasting in a store window for cash. After several days he displayed a sign to the effect that he no longer felt hungry. Nevertheless, he was starving.

What is meant by "righteousness," which nowadays is an unattractive word? Not what we call "justice," "an eye for an eye." If an assailant blinds you, he cannot restore your sight. He may be sent to jail but is probably a worse man on release. So by the course of "justice" everybody loses, justice being a woman holding scales which she cannot read because she is blindfolded. Jesus said flatly that our justice soon becomes injustice: "Unless your righteousness exceeds that of the scribes and Pharisees," it is merely "an eye for an eye," an equation which is always broken. So the New English Bible is true both in the text and in the footnote. The text reads, "thirst to see right prevail," meaning by "right" the goodwill that finds us in Christ. Some folks agonize over the brutality of war, the dinginess of slums, and the stuffiness of many a church. They agonize more over the blindness which says only, "We must keep the law—'an eye for an eye.'" The footnote reads, "or to do what is right." Yes, they "hunger and thirst" (not tepid words) for the true man to be formed in themselves. For whenever we yearn for a gentler earth, one question places us under instant arrest: "What have I done?" What a blessing that Christ does not ask for the deed, but only for the deep-down longing! For corporate sin is a dark lake fed by the poison of individual sin.

Then what of the amazing promise: "They shall be satisfied"? Those who hunger for the true man to be formed in them, knowing their helplessness, cast themselves on God with their eyes on Christ and so find pardon. The New Testament strikes home to the human problem: "Not having a right-eousness of my own, . . . but that which is through faith in Christ." As for those who thirst for goodwill on earth, spring keeps breaking through, though only their eyes can see it. God leashes evil. The lecher is never "satisfied"; he comes on nausea. The miser likewise; soon he is hard like his coins. We may note here the fact that faith in Christ in his day foresaw heaven as the banquet of the Messiah where earth's hunger and thirst are satisfied. Yet since heaven fills earth, God's hungry ones know his present grace and are always being satisfied.

Blessed are the merciful . . .

"Blessed are the merciful." In the Old Testament *"mercy"* roots (where else?) in God's clemency toward captives and finds flower in his readiness to forgive. In the New Testament, Christ himself gives meaning to every beatitude: his kind of mercy. So our mercy is not charity which is no better than giving a quarter to a beggar, but concern for earth's stricken folk and our quickness to forgive our enemies. Christ lived in a cruel world. Whole nations were made captive without mercy. What kind of mind thought up death by crucifixion? Many a Jew then believed that all pain was punishment—why try to relieve it? Romans despised mercy.

Greek Stoics met pain with fortitude which forgot their neighbors. In some lands ailing folk were simply carried into the forest to die.

What of our time? We show a measure of mercy: we have hospitals and community chests. But we have hunger across the world and the blind bombing of whole cities. Has there ever been such wholesale cruelty? Merciful people are suspect; they are do-gooders whose activity may be against the national interest. We should not blink to the fact that our mercy now takes a corporate cast through civic and national agencies. Our boasted technology, to cite only one instance, has largely cut off unskilled labor. Thus the need for a massive plan of education for semi-skilled tasks. We may not like this "new socialism" (I myself do not laugh aloud), but technology brings factories, and they bring cities, and they bring an inevitably corporate life. Yet the need for private mercy is always with us. The other day I heard a man solve the problem of the ghetto by saying, "I've always been able to earn a good living." That remark reveals at best a blind mind and at worst a stony heart. How would you spend a million dollars? That question was asked in open contest, and the prize went to a man who replied in effect: "I would try to be the Good Samaritan as I go down the road." That answer, though far from complete, is a fine affair.

Meanwhile each of us must plead for mercy, if only for failing in mercy. Our angry young men nowadays rail at the cruelty of our world or become atheists, and we are all tempted to debit God with the pain and credit ourselves with a mercy rarely practiced. God has given us freedom so to judge him. But are we wise enough? Can we see far enough? Are our hands clean enough? The criminal still festers in outmoded jails where "justice" too often deepens his need. The pathetic bunch of flowers on a neighbor's door still goes unnoticed.

"But we do not know them," is the poor excuse. Maybe nobody can know anybody except through mercy given and received. Therefore all of us in our suffering echo the word of Christ: "Blessed are the merciful."

"For they shall obtain mercy," but not as a reward. Mercy is not for sale. It is not a matter of you get as good as you give (what a hell if that were true of man or God!). He does not keep books with red ink and black ink, fortunately for our failures. He is not bribed. The merciful enter a secret world, an ever oncoming springtime, and never know until they feel on their faces the warmth of a green equinox. Tennyson has a doctor asking, "Can prayer set a broken bone?" and muttering, "The good Lord Jesus has had his day." The poet makes answer in the nurse's thoughts:

Had? has it come? It has only dawned. It will
    come by and by.
O, how could I serve in the wards if the hope
    of the world were a lie?

The merciful find a hope that is firmer than doubt and stronger than all cruelty.

Blessed are the pure in heart . . .

"Blessed are the pure in heart." It is strange indeed that this favorite beatitude should also be the most unapproachable. For who is pure in heart? That heaven is far beyond our upreaching hands. The word "pure" occurs twenty-eight times in the New Testament. It is variously translated as "white" linen, "clear" glass, "unalloyed" gold. The word may have two primary meanings. One is cleanliness in the inner parts, not in regard to sex only, but to any other seduction or sordidness. Our present revolt against Victorian "puritanism" has a strong case, for we now know that an angular moralism (not morality) injures both the censor and

his victims; repression brings sickness of mind. But there is need now for a sharp rejoinder; the present rampant impuritanism is no cure for puritanism. An uninhibited man in our cult of sex and blood hardly offers a convincing answer to repression. So this beatitude stands.

But the other meaning of "pure" may be more central: singleness of purpose toward God. "Motivation" is not the word, even though it is a cliché in our time. For who can trace a man's motives? No psychiatrist can claim that gift; he would need to know the whole human record. Besides, motivation has an inward-turning eye while purity of heart looks outward toward God disclosed in Christ. This singleness is primary; it yields to no secondary god such as science or democracy. Without this singleness science becomes destruction and democracy an atomized chaos. No wayside altar entices the pure in heart; they are on pilgrimage to that throne which is yet as *lowly as a cross. Jesus pleaded for the single eye. We must confess that our motives are always mixed. But the pure do not live to scrutinize their motives. They trust the world of motive to the forgiving grace of God and fix their gaze and their obedience on Christ.*

Then what is meant by "see God"? The words themselves invite dismay. Indeed the Bible in the Old Testament tells us that no man shall see God and live, and in the New Testament that "no one has ever seen God." Mortal flesh would shrivel in his light. So "see" cannot here mean physical seeing. We must take a further step: this beatitude does not guarantee an unbroken assurance of God's presence; there is too much human dust for that clear heaven. Actually we cannot "see" even our best friend, much less "see" God. The promise is promise ("shall see"), not present fulfillment. But the pure in heart have present glimpses, foregleams which are themselves the pledge of the coming day. Meanwhile they see our present world with new eyes, so that even the bloody hatreds of our time are no disproof of God but by terrible inversion are the sign of his judgment, which is the other side of love's shield. The pure find God in the lowliest tasks, as Brother Lawrence found God among pots and pans, and give thanks that a cosmic sun glints on the commonest table. They sing their "Holy, holy, holy" in all seasons, for they know, though sometimes only when God has passed by, that the whole earth is filled with his glory. They ask no reward, or they would not be pure in heart. Singleness of heart is its own heaven.

Blessed are the peacemakers . . .

"Blessed are the peacemakers." This beatitude involves more than the patching up of personal quarrels. We blunder if we describe (and dismiss?) these "Blesseds" as a "merely individualistic ethic." Jesus did not peddle platitudes to hermits. He addressed his nation both as to its own national witness and as to its dealings with the hated Roman and the despised Gentile. So "peace" here concerns both our private grudges and our world wars. In the Bible the word "peace" lives on a veritical line. It is first, peace with God, for without that there can be no peace among men. But that does not mean that when a man finds peace with

God his work is done; it has only begun. This sharp word must be written: if evangelism does not lead to brave witness in our world of affairs, it may sink into self-indulgence. Indeed evangelism by the very meaning of the word is the sharing of a joy. The accurate translation of the Christmas promise is not the usual "good will to men," or the much worse "among men of goodwill" (when did we qualify?); the meaning is: "Glory to God in highest heaven [because] he has now shown his goodwill toward men." How easy to make war! One shot and the battle is begun. How hard to make peace! War feeds our angers and pride;

peace asks lowliness, patience, buffeting (a second blow on the cheek after the first blow is accepted), and many a pondered strategy. A department of war is a cinch; we have no department of peace because that would spell too hard a task. So we have peacehopers and peacetalkers but few peacemakers. War does not end war; it sows the dragon's teeth of new wars. It does not stop communism, but offers it the fertile ground of desolation, as witness the burgeoning of communism after each of the world wars. It does not promote democracy, but invites the strong man to rule the resultant chaos. If there is any bright lining to war's thunder and lightning it is this: the bloody futility becomes clearer with every new conflict. Thus in the Vietnam War an officer exclaimed after the battle for Hill 875: "I don't care anymore if I get back to the world, a world too stupid to stay out of war, too stupid to know how to fight it, too stupid to know how to end it." But of course he cannot escape the world and should not try. The church deplores war in general but almost endorses each particular war. If the church would live, it must become outrightly the peacemaker.

"God shall call them his sons." (NEB.) The word "sons" in the writings of the Old Testament prophets meant those who keep God's covenant. Thus Hosea: "It shall be said to them, 'Sons of the living God.'" In the New Testament the covenant is through the Christ event: "This is my blood of the new covenant." Every beatitude lives in his light. "Sons of God"—what a title! The very God adopting a mortal man! "My peace," said Christ, "I give [bequeath] to you." He said it in the shadow of Calvary. So peace is not our reward. It is always on the vertical line, a legacy written in his will. When someone suggested to Richard Cobden, who labored for disarmament even in his day, that he might be famous enough to be buried in Westminster Abbey, he answered: "I hope not; my spirit would not be at rest among those men of war." Thus another sharp comment on the church's endorsement of war. The church will be renewed, but not on present terms. Christ has his own "Abbey." There the peacemakers are honored, for they accept scorn in a new kind of courage. They who look back as "Sons of the living God" shall know that "spring came on forever."

52

Blessed are those who are persecuted for righteousness' sake . . .

"Blessed are those who are persecuted for righteousness' sake." Christ's words are not tame. Sometimes, as here, they stab us wide awake and prompt our incredulous "No!" Before we try to understand the link between "happy" and "persecuted," we should note the honest realism: Christ warns that his followers will be maligned and stricken. He never hides the sharp flint. Our colleges hail the "dignity of man," but Pascal was more candid; he spoke about "the grandeur and misery of man." Much of the misery comes from man's tragicomic attempt to be his own small god. Thus the faith-full are hated and reproached. As far as we know, only one of the Apostles died in his bed. Some of them were crucified. Paul's pilgrimage reads like one long torture chamber. "To the lions!" is the cry raised against lowly men of faith. Jesus flatly issued that warning.

Our time is no exception. Peacemakers, who as such can have no truck with communism, are called "dupes of the communists." The advocate of civil rights is not popular in his suburb. Preachers are being pressured: rich men with static minds withdraw their subscriptions if the preacher displeases them. That fact is a sign of hope, for the church of late has been so tepid that nobody thought it worth the trouble of persecution. Of course the persecuted man is no masochist. He gives no place to either a martyr complex or any self-pity, for he is enlisted in the cause of right. The Beatitudes are not tame. They cannot be domesticated or brought to heel. They invite persecution in a world in which the devil never lacks for followers.

But the persecuted should "leap for joy." Why? Because they now belong in the exultant order of the prophets who as a "cloud of witnesses" watch and cheer our earthly course. Their bright company lives in a gladness better than that of the Round Table of King Arthur's knights. The persecuted have an even greater reason for sheer gladness—"for theirs is the kingdom of heaven." Clearly Christ believed in the resurrection of the dead. In that issue he sided with the Pharisees against the unbelieving Sadducees. Has not Christ proved the Resurrection? At any rate we cannot get rid of him. In a contest to decide who are the happiest people the prevailing answers were these: a surgeon performing a crucial operation with success, a craftsman busy at his task, a mother crooning over her baby. A friend has suggested even a better answer: Joan of Arc in her martyr flames suddenly crying, "Lord Jesus!" The best answer is: Christ facing his cross in joy and bequeathing joy to us. "Persecuted" saves us from the current sentimentalism: "Be kind to others, and they will be kind to you." The kindest man who ever lived was strung up by his hands. But "persecuted" points us nevertheless to a certain gladness which always lives at the heart of oppression dared and accepted for Christ's sake.

This too brief journey through the Beatitudes fulfills W. H. Auden's word:

He is the Way.
Follow Him through the Land of Unlikeness;
You will see rare beasts, and have unique
    adventures.

The Beatitudes are certainly "unlike," and any man daring to live them will have "unique adventures." The "Blesseds" are in poetic form. One scholar contends that in Christ's original Aramaic they had both rhyme and rhythm. So they are not aphorisms or philosophy or good counsel, but jets of flame from an always burning heart. They are not relevant to our culture if that now fashionable adjective means "easily related to"; they are springtime breaking through the "winter of our discontent." We do not believe them. That is why we could not call our earth a happy place. Christ lifts his gentle banner. You and I are invited to engage in the secret jousts where we know that "spring came on forever."

Compare the Beatitudes with the Ten Commandments. The latter are not a barracks' edict, for they are set in the context of God's covenant with men. But they prescribe, enjoin, and in some instances forbid. The "Blesseds," on the other hand, invite us to joy. They are not a time-bound ethic, but open to every tomorrow. They honor our freedom; we are asked to decide the quality of mercy in our new, mechanized time. Matthew rounds off the sharp edge of Luke's version, changes Luke's second person (Happy are you) to the safer third person (Happy are they who), and omits Luke's "woes."

But the two accounts are not in contradiction. Matthew's "poor in spirit," for instance, drives Luke's blunt "poor" to clearer and deeper meaning while Luke's "Woe to you" is not a curse; it warns and pities.

There is one question which we cannot honestly sidestep. It comes full force whenever we ponder the opposites of the several Beatitudes: the proud, the callous, the aggressors, and the rest. They are a baleful, horrifying company. So the question: Why are we born into such a planet? Why the call for the Beatitudes? Our earth is a realm of contradiction. The company of the "Blesseds" is surrounded and beset by evil men and evil systems. The snake always befouls the garden. If Christ is God's creative thrust through whom the worlds were made (such is the tremendous New Testament faith), why is our earth and every man in it torn by civil war? The Beatitudes themselves raise that agonizing question, and there is no schoolroom answer. So we grope and

61

guess. Maybe only in such an earth can we vote for Christ in brave freewill. Maybe only in mystery can we find meaning—where else? Maybe only in a realm of contradictions can we know our need of God and be found of him, and thus know ourselves. Maybe only in civil war can we offer God an unperjured faith and an unbribed devotion. Our minds cannot find any final answer, for our minds are finite and always clouded by human dust.

Christ has blazed the trail and is himself the answer. To those who would follow he is both pardon and pledge. All the battalions of evil converged to slay him and fell back broken, for springtime streamed from an open grave. The "Hallelujah Chorus" was not inspired by a lie. There is no academic answer either to "the mystery of lawlessness" or the miracle of the saints. If there were, it would not help us. The devils presumably know the intention of their Adversary, but they also "fear and tremble"—because they are devils. The answer is in the venture of the Beatitudes. Then we shall know not in any poor logic, but in the heart's invincible persuasions. So Auden again:

He is the Life.
Love Him in the World of the Flesh;
And at your marriage all its occasions shall
    dance for joy.

Beyond death a Man may meet us on a quiet road, and if the devil has tripped us, he may say: "Why did you give me that answer on earth?" But if we have tried his way, where in grace our yearning intentions are taken for the deed, he may greet us with his own beatitude word: "Come, O blessed of my Father, inherit the kingdom prepared for you from the foundation of the world." Then we shall understand that even in our torn and ambiguous earth "spring came on forever."

ILLUSTRATIONS: Etchings by Diana Blank

DESIGN: Diana Blank

TYPE: Optima Italic—10 pt., leaded 5 pts.

TYPESETTER: The Parthenon Press

MANUFACTURER: The Parthenon Press

PRINTING PROCESS: Offset, 2 colors

PAPER: Body, 70 lb. Beckett Text Laid, India
        Graham Paper Company

        End Sheets, 80 lb. Andorra Text, Cinnamon
        Weyerhaeuser Company

BINDING MATERIAL: Fictionette, Natural Finish 3265
                  The Columbia Mills, Inc.